AUTISM
Respecting difference

An inside view of autism for carers,
professionals and families

Phoebe Caldwell
Illustrated by Jodie Zutt

Autism – Respecting difference

An inside view of autism for carers, professionals and families

Published by:
Pavilion Publishing and Media Ltd
Blue Sky Offices, 25 Cecil Pashley Way
Shoreham by Sea, West Sussex
BN43 5FF

Tel: 01273 434 943
Email: info@pavpub.com
Web: www.pavpub.com

Published 2022

A catalogue record for this book is available from the British Library.

ISBN: 978-1-803881-57-7

Pavilion Publishing and Media is a leading publisher of books, training materials and digital content in mental health, social care and allied fields. Pavilion and its imprints offer must-have knowledge and innovative learning solutions underpinned by sound research and professional values.

Author: Phoebe Caldwell and Jodie Zutt
Illustrations: Jodie Zutt
Cover design: Emma Dawe, Pavilion Publishing and Media Ltd
Page layout and typesetting: Tony Pitt, Pavilion Publishing and Media Ltd
Printing: CMP Digital Print Solutions

Dedication

Autism: Respecting Difference spans forty-five years of work, and I am no longer in touch with many of the people who have shared their lives with me and who appear in this book. Some have died and some moved. At the time of our work together, permission was granted to use relevant material. Names have been altered. What remains is the essence of our interactions.

Phoebe

This book by Jodie and Phoebe is dedicated to Hayden, from whom we continue to learn.

Contents

Part One:
The Brainworld of Autism

Which of us is autistic?

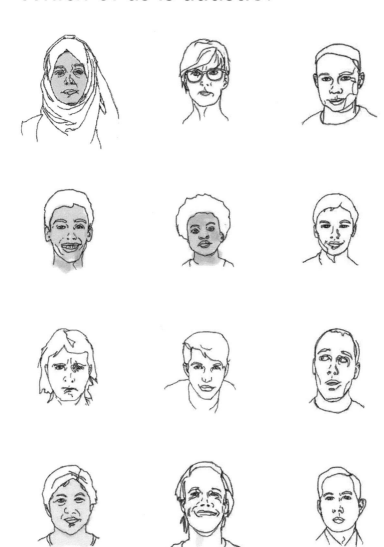

Lemmy sits at his computer, playing the same clip over and over again.

"I'm different from all you guys. I'm different from all you guys!"

So, is there a difference?

Starting with ourselves:

While we can learn from the outside what it is to think like another person, it is very difficult for us to pick up on how they **feel**.

Most pages of this small book have a cartoon. These are designed to help us feel (sense) how the person with autism is experiencing the world, and the link between these feelings and 'difficult-to-manage' behaviours.

I will try to avoid technical terms where possible.

Just as all people are different, the nerve pain that is part of an autistic experience is described differently by different people on the autistic spectrum. The feelings are internal: nobody outside feels what is going on inside.

Welcome to the brainworld of autism

The Australian writer and artist Donna Williams said of her experience of autism:

"There was a rip through the centre of my soul. Self-abuse was the outward sign of an earthquake nobody saw. I was like an appliance during a power surge. As I blew fuses my hands pulled out my hair and slapped my face. My teeth bit my flesh like an animal bites the bars of its cage, not realising the cage was my body. My legs ran round in manic circles, as though they could outrun the body they were attached to. My head hit whatever was next to it like someone trying to crack a nut that had grown too large for its shell. There was an overwhelming feeling of inner deafness – deafness to self that would consume all that was left in a fever pitch of silent screaming."

The Swedish author and lecturer Gunilla Gerland describes it differently:

"All the time I was growing up there was a constant shudder down my spine... it was a constant torture, especially when it changed in intensity. It was like cold steel down my spine, hard and fluid at the same time, with a metallic finger drumming the outside. Like sharp clips in my spine and lemonade inside. Icy heat and digging fiery cold... like the sound of screeching chalk on the blackboard turned into a silent concentration of feeling placed on the back of my neck. From there, so metallic, the feeling radiated out into my arms. Clipped itself into my elbows, but never came to an end, never came to an end."[1]

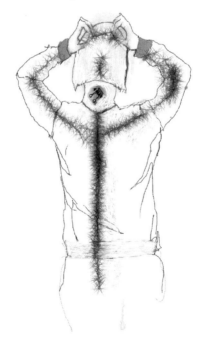

---

1   Gerland, G. (2003) *A Real Person: Life on the Outside.* London: Souvenir Press.

Mis-wired connections in the **brain** lead to

sensory processing problems

Sensory overload and **anxiety**

feed each other

triggering **pain**

and

distress behaviours

aggression towards **self** or **others**

flight

meltdowns

shutdowns

Anything to put a distance between themselves and the (rightly or wrongly) perceived source of the sensory overload.

Autism research has traditionally focused on behaviour, describing the condition as a triad of impairments: problems with communication, imagination and the ability to engage in social contexts. More recent studies, however, have focused on what is happening in the brain to trigger these effects.

Autistic or not, how we behave and how we respond to the world is determined by our genes. All of us are different. We look different, we behave differently. Some of us find the world easy to understand. Others of us, especially those on the autistic spectrum, struggle.

So is a small boy correct when he says this to me?

"My brain's not wired up properly."

Is there something different in the way messages are being passed around the brain, which makes it more difficult for people on the autistic spectrum to work out what is happening?

Is the message that should be going from A to B getting lost on the way?

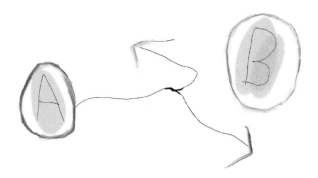

Problems with connections

Our brains are amazing. Thanks to modern science we can now look inside our heads and see that this is the case.[2]

We make sense of our environment by connecting sensory images and messages from the world outside with how we feel inside.

Our sensory organs (eyes, ears, etc.) may be working perfectly well. For example, if we go to an optician for an eye test, our vision may be fine.

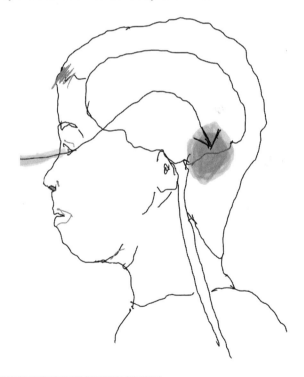

---

2   Video of cortical neurons available at:
https://www.youtube.com/watch?v = irdqVhzG4SQ.

When we sense something, if all is well, the sense organ sends the message to the correct processing area, which forwards the message to relevant parts of the brain – to assess whether what we see (or sense) is threatening, build a story and work out how we should respond.

In the autistic brain, the trouble starts with connections between nerve cells (neurons), which carry what we see 'out there' from the eye to the visual processing area at the back of the brain. This is the same with sounds being carried from the ear to the auditory processing area, or smell from the nose, taste from the mouth, pressure and touch.

If the connections between our nerve cells are not linked up along the most effective route, messages will be sent around the brain in all directions. They may end up at the wrong destinations or abort. This is very stressful, as the brain desperately fires off trying to work out what is going on.

Stress builds up and the brain teeters on the edge of a meltdown. And since there are roughly the same number of branching nerve cells in our brain as stars in the Milky Way (who counted?!) and trillions of connections (synapses), there is plenty of scope for error.

Whether we are autistic or not, all of us have some misconnections and mis-wiring. For the non-autistic person, these are mis-routings that do not affect how our brains process in a way that has an impact on our comprehension: the important messages follow a direct route and do not get lost. Some people will also have hardwired special talents, both in autistic and non-autistic brains. Some messages will get mis-routed and lost, however.

This 'mis-routing' goes right back to problems in development, set off by 'fragile genes' (genes with parts that get lost or damaged). Much of this damage is done before we are born.

Autism may be either inherited or caused by environmental circumstances affecting a parent. In some children it may only become apparent later on, when the glial cells (the brain's special domestic service) become overenthusiastic and cut away too many of the connections between cells, or are lazy and don't tidy up enough, leaving an excess of unused pathways cluttering up the system.

This 'deep cleaning' usually happens around the age of three. The severity of autism varies, depending on where the damage occurs. People can be autistic at any level of cognitive ability. Every autistic person is different. Some may be great artists or musicians: even the great mathematician Albert Einstein is thought to have been on the autistic spectrum.

However, others will struggle with any sort of intellectual and/or social activity. It all depends on where the misconnections are, and where messages are getting lost.

Connectivity problems and consequent distress behaviours are not character deficits

Autism can turn up in anyone – not just other families. It can turn up in our children.

Faulty connections may affect any part of the brain. If the wiring is defective in any way, it is difficult to assemble a coherent picture of our surroundings. It's like a *mis-wiring* at the telephone exchange; the confusion makes it difficult for the person to know what is going on around them. Activities that seem normal to a non-autistic person may be literally terrifying.

The person lives on red alert, always on the lookout for something to go wrong and trigger the pain.

To repeat: There may be too many links between nerve cells or too few, or the connections may be heading in the wrong direction. This applies not only to incoming sensory pathways to the brain (the ones we usually think of: taste, smell, hearing, sight, touch and external pressure), but also feelings from our bodily organs (our stomach, heart etc.) and temperature.

Synaesthesia

Messages coming in through one sense organ may be sent to the wrong processing area. Sound messages, for example, may be sent to the visual processing area. Then the person may 'see' sounds (synaesthesia). This can be very confusing and, in different forms, is fairly common in people on the autistic spectrum.

A child likes to bite babies.[3] The louder they yell, the happier she is. Rather than being a 'bad girl', she is seeing their screams as beautiful moving rainbows of light; a personalised laser show. It is even better when her mother shouts at her. Described as synaesthetic, she cannot understand why people try to stop her.

3   Johansson, I. (2007) *A Different Childhood: Autism from the Inside.* Inkwell Books.

Autistic children and adults may not get the same
volume of incoming messages as we do, and can
experience sound, especially sudden noises, like the
sensation of a dog barking.

The brain desperately fires off, trying to make out
what is happening – a state which can be truly
physically agonising. Other people will apparently
love the sound of a washing machine and sit beside it,
using it to drown out other frequencies.

People may try different ways to separate
themselves from the source of the sensory overload.
They are looking to give themselves space to sort
out the confusion so that the brain does not go into
complete meltdown.

The overloaded autistic person may try to separate themselves from others by lashing out, scratching, spitting or pinching, in the hope that the source of their sensory overload (me or you) will go away.

Or they may try to escape by running away.

Or they will focus on a particular activity such as rocking, playing with their fingers, or lining up cars – or having what we call 'one-track minds', persistently thinking about a particular subject. (This is known as 'stimming'.) Outsiders may find this irritating and try to stop the activity, when they should be looking for ways of reducing the sensory overload that is triggering it.

Each person has their own way of responding to overwhelming stress. Basil says:

"*My head is running away, my head is running away.*"

Finally, the brain may simply shut itself down so that the body stops responding.

Even here, there is variation. Sometimes the trigger sets off a response and sometimes not, so the person may be labelled as lazy.

Think:

Imagine you have a bad fall and knock yourself out.
Apart from the pain when you come round, you may
be concussed and the world seems to be spinning.
What if it was always like this? Or imagine trying to
live in a kaleidoscope where the pattern never settles.
You are always trying to grapple with floating bits.
Or it may feel like a lion roaring or a Catherine wheel
whizzing round in your head.

Care providers may find it difficult to manage these
behaviours, but for the autistic person the overactivity
in their brain can be catastrophic. As they struggle
to keep up with the flood of incoming stimuli, most
people retreat into their own world of repetitive
behaviour or cut off completely.

**In order to help, we need to downsize the
environmental stimuli that are triggering hyper-
(over) and hypo- (under) sensitivities, setting
off sensory overload and causing the difficult-to-
manage 'distress behaviours'.**

What are these underlying sensory problems?

The sense that is affected depends on where the links
in the brain are not joined up.

Sight

Many people on the autistic spectrum have Irlen Syndrome distortions – not in the eyes themselves, but in the visual processing system. Everything may break into fragments and float around.

This is caused by bright light (certain very specific frequencies), intricate patterns and particular colours. Some autistic people will try to avoid these: pulling the curtains, darkening the room. Or the person will keep their head down, shade their eyes, turn a dimmer switch right down. Black-and-white patterns are particularly confusing.

When the person is becoming sensorily overloaded, if they cannot dim the trigger they may become so desperate that they attack other people or themselves – banging their head or self-harming in other ways. We see this as aggression rather than desperation.

As well as visual distortions, Irlen Syndrome can affect mood, balance and sleep patterns, as well as setting off difficult-to-manage 'distress behaviours'.

Mike only sits in a corner, tearing up paper. He does not engage with his family. He eats little and will not go out. When I put on a blue light, he puts down the paper, comes over, takes my hand, looks deeply into my eyes, then takes his mother's hand and smiles at her. He starts to manipulate the coloured light control. When we give him a blue plate, he eats up his food. When we give him a blue coat, he goes outside calmly. When Mike sees blue, he knows what he is seeing. It has meaning for him and helps him to define himself as separate from the world outside. He knows what he is doing.

A six-year-old boy was in the low-ability class at school until I noticed that he blinked whenever he looked out of the window. An Irlen test sent him back with blue lenses. The school realised that he was very clever and bored with what he was being offered. Subsequently, he was sent to a school for gifted children.

In the same way that some teachers did not originally believe in dyslexia, there are still many people who do not believe in the reality of Irlen Syndrome. This is because it is so difficult for us to understand that other people's perceptions may be different from our own. When Donna Williams found the right colour lenses (pink ones, in her case), she said:

> "Oh my God, it's as if the whole world went shunt. Everything stopped floating around. That's what the rest of the world is seeing."

Apart from visual processing, Irlen Syndrome can also cause balance and sleep problems.

Unrecognised Irlen syndrome may underlie a lot of grief. A child is excluded from school because he is in distress and throws a chair. His teacher is unaware that his 'difficult-to-manage' behaviour is triggered by the environment. Fluorescent strip lighting, for example, is very painful; real agony.

To spot Irlen Syndrome:

Look and see if the autistic child or adult avoids bright light, squints as they look out of the window, closes the curtains, or wants to wear a cap outdoors.

Does the person have problems with patterns which are too complicated to sort out? A man tried to strip his support worker when they were wearing a black-and-white striped T-shirt. He stopped at once when they wore a plain one.

Ask yourself: Does the person have favourite colours, choose to be in a room painted in those colours, or avoid certain colours, getting upset when they are exposed to them? Any of these signs suggest Irlen Syndrome and require testing by a trained professional (rather than an optician, who uses a machine for testing) to see which frequency of light is causing the problem and recommend specific tinted lenses.[4] It is a very specific frequency. Any old colour will not do.

Comparative scans of a child working on the same activity with and without Irlen tinted glasses show the confusion in the brain when their visual processing difficulty is not being addressed.

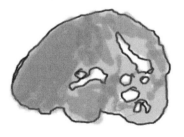

Diagrammatic representation of SPECT scans from the Amen Clinics, California, USA. Left: Brain overactivity when visual processing difficulties are uncorrected. Right: Brain activity when the visual processing difficulty is corrected with appropriate tinted lenses.[5]

---

4   Tina Yates: info@irleneast.com

5   See page 28 of Caldwell, P. et al. (2019) *Responsive Communication: Combining attention to sensory issues with using body language (intensive interaction) to interact with autistic adults and children.* Pavilion Publishing and Media.

Hints:

Paint walls and ceilings (which reflect light) dark –
preferably dark versions of the individual's favourite
colour.

Use tinted glass in windows. You may need tinted
windows in a car to cut down the amount of visual
processing as the car moves.

Wear plain-coloured, dark clothes. Avoid logos.

Above all, avoid fluorescent strip lighting. Use
dimmer switches so that the autistic person can
adjust the light level.

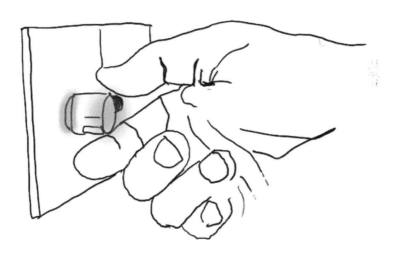

Sound

For children and adults, hypersensitivity (over-sensitivity) to sound can be a massive problem – like a tidal wave, especially in crowded rooms. For some autistic children, sound at school may be so overwhelming that they will do anything (even self-injure) to avoid having to attend. Voices overlap, meaning that classrooms, corridors and assembly halls, break times, and changeover times in respite homes are particular problems. A single voice may be unbelievably harsh. Sudden sounds like dogs barking can be terrifying and painful.

Roddy will not let anyone into his house without having a meltdown. I stand at the open door where he can see me and put my finger to my mouth, and then point inside to show him I will speak quietly. Once he understands this, he beckons me inside.

A small boy pushes his mother away. Her voice is hard and loud. He keeps trying to jump off the table onto his head and needs the intervention of four care staff to prevent this. There is a certain frequency in his mother's voice which is hurting him badly and he pushes her away. He stops at once when I suggest to her that she speak to him softly. Now he invites her to be with him to read him stories.

Some autistic people with sound processing problems are assisted by noise-cancelling headphones – a good-quality pair rather than cheap builder's ear defenders which cut out all sound completely. Noise-cancelling headphones allow close-up speech to be heard and reduce ambient noise. These are particularly useful in class.

Mary used to take her work and sit under her desk, pulling chairs around her to lessen the confusion. She was given some noise-cancelling headphones. After half an hour, her teachers came and said:

"We had no idea how clever she is. Within half an hour, her ability went through the roof. We had to move her up to a higher-level class."

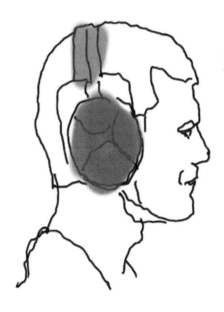

All those who support the child or adult need to understand the importance of ensuring that they have the headphones available. This will cut down the anxiety and stress which build up and trigger distress behaviour.

It may be enough for the child to have their headphones on the desk so they can put them on if it gets noisy, rather than wearing them all the time. However, staff need to understand that these are vital aids to learning, and make sure they are accessible.

We cannot assess the level of a child's ability until we have addressed their sensory difficulties.

Most pupils want to learn in class with their peers, but some may be unable to cope with the sensory overload and may only be able to learn in a quiet room.

Taste and smell

Taste and smell may be difficult to address because the source is diffuse. Generally, it is a question of avoidance or very gradually building up tolerance (which is not easy). It may be a question of texture; how food feels in the mouth. Some people love crunchy food; others hate it because it hurts or because the sound of chewing hurts.

When Mike would only eat from a blue plate, he was not 'being difficult': he could only eat off a colour where he could see what he was doing. Another child would only eat from a grey plate. A young woman with synaesthesia would throw her plate on the floor, saying she could not eat her pudding because it was "too black".

The visual distortions caused by certain frequencies of light mean that the 'wrong' colour is causing the brain to overload, which is distressing or painful.

Smell is difficult to anticipate. Avoid wearing scents and using fragranced products. Remember that the autistic person may be so sensitive to smells, that overload is triggered by the soap you used yesterday.

The reaction of a young man is so strong, he vomits when his mother opens the fridge which has egg sandwiches inside.

Touch

Autistic people may be oversensitive to touch. This is different to over-sensitivity or under-sensitivity to pressure.

"Touch feels like spiders crawling out of my skin."

Touch sensitivity may even extend to proximity without contact. Having someone close behind you can set off spinal pain. A child may be unable to concentrate if there is another desk behind them; they need to sit with their back to the wall.

Showers may be painful:

*"A shower feels like red-hot needles being fired
at me."*

Some people will strip because the friction of clothes
may be painful, or they only feel comfortable with the
air on their skin. If this is the case, they need to be
given adequate privacy.

Try very lightweight clothes such as silk.

Pressure

Pressure messages from the outside world help our brain to work out its position and determine the boundaries between what is 'me' and 'not me'.

Due to linkage problems in the nerve pathways, many autistic people do not get good pressure messages from the outside world. These get lost somewhere before they reach the areas in the brain telling the person where they are, what they are doing, and – because this affects their sense of place and boundary – what is 'me' and what is 'not me'. Even who they are is blurred.

So they may try to give themselves extra-deep feedback: banging their feet, scrunching their toes, walking on tiptoe.

They may scratch themselves, squeeze their fingers or bang their heads. This is interpreted as self-injury, but is rather a desperate attempt to increase the feedback from the outside world and reduce the brain's confusion.

Joe jumps up and down all the time and it irritates people. When he visits a psychiatrist, she tells him that when he leaves her room, he must never jump again. Joe is a good boy and stops jumping, but, he says, "At the instant I left that room, I lost my sense of self."[6]

6   *Being Autistic.* Autscape.

Without boundaries, other people can feel confusing and invasive, so autistic people may fence themselves in to create a boundary with the outside world they fear.

Some children will walk around the playground beating the fence so they know where it is. Or they may even look into a framed reflection to try and set up a boundary.

Almost all behaviours make sense if looked at in terms of sensory processing and sensitivities.

Hugs

In order to receive the pressure feedback they crave, some people are desperate for hugs and will grab anyone who approaches and try to engulf them. If they are rejected, they come back again and again for what they need to confirm their embodiment.

The pressure helps these people know where they are and what their boundaries are. My own response when I come into their space is to immediately hold out my arms and give them a big hug with lots of pressure, and then disengage. This usually satisfies their need.

It is easy to misinterpret the motives underlying other people's behaviour, as with the man who was trying to strip his key worker when she was wearing a striped T-shirt. His care workers were about to send for a psychiatrist or the police. The problem stopped when I suggested that she wear a plain T-shirt.

Another autistic man who had no sight would try to grab his female support workers by the breast. I pointed out that when they approached him, he was reaching out for support rather than sexual contact and the breast was the nearest part of their body. When they came to him from the side, he would take their arm and off they'd go.

Hope did not feel in touch with the ground: she said it felt as if she was floating around in a balloon.[7]

Hope knew when she was walking, but could not feel the ground. So if she felt she was getting stressed, she would curl up her toes inside her shoes to have something to focus on. Using textured insoles inside her trainers gave her better feedback.[8] Her ability to relate to the world has improved beyond all recognition:

"It helps to stop or lessen overload. I now feel the bumps on the reflexology insoles, which is stress relieving and calming."

7   Caldwell, P. et al. (2019) *Responsive Communication: Combining attention to sensory issues with using body language (intensive interaction) to interact with autistic adults and children.* Pavilion Publishing and Media Ltd.

8   Textured insoles available at: https://revsstore.com/

Hope's brother is non-verbal and shy. We tried a pair of insoles in his trainers, and he gave a big grin and thumbs up when he put them on.

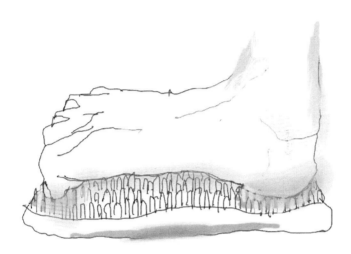

When Paul Isaacs[9] tried the textured insoles, he said:

"I have noticed a better sense of body connectivity, a better stride, gait and locomotion, my posture has improved, and I'm not slamming my feet on the ground trying to get input: my hemiplegia has greatly benefited (my right side)."

---

9   Paul Isaacs is an autistic trainer, speaker, consultant and blogger. He has co-authored books including *Life through a Kaleidoscope* (2013: Chipmunka Publishing).

Other aids to increasing physical feedback include:

- an AstroTurf mat on the floor

- a pogo stick

- vibration

- regular trampoline sessions several times a day

- swings

- cycling

- weightlifting

- running with a backpack full of cans

Richard says that when he is cycling, he has five points of pressure that let him know where he is. Even when he is lecturing, he has one hand on his bike.

These activities need to be programmed into the day; they are not recreational but are providing essential feedback, telling the person what they are doing.

Emotional overload

It is often said that people with autism do not have emotions. This is incorrect. The problem is regulating emotions.

Sometimes they appear to lack empathy with other people; sometimes their feelings may be completely over the top.

Emotional overload may be triggered by any form of emotional warmth. Christmas and birthdays can often be upsetting.

Sometimes the trigger is more subtle.

Dave found people using his name too intrusive and was upset when he even heard other names. I suggested that we email each other and use our initials: 'D' and 'P'. It was as though an enormous weight had been lifted off him.

Avoid anything that focuses individual attention on the person, such as praise. Any acknowledgement of something positive needs to be casual. Advice from an autistic teacher was to play it cool and say as you walk out of the room:

"That seemed to go very well."

Or:

"That was good."

Rather than the direct:

"Well done. Good work."

Another way in which the autistic person protects themselves is to develop a 'mask' between themselves and the person they are talking to, but this is a strain and the mask may give way suddenly.

Sensory overload causes anxiety, and anxiety enhances sensory overload, in a vicious spiral.

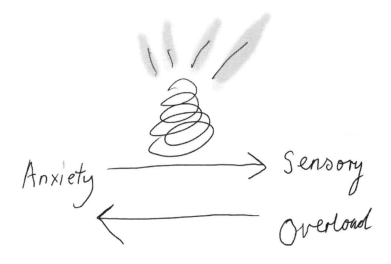

Distress behaviour *always* indicates sensory overload.

The more anxious the person is, the more sensitive they will feel. Conversely, the more sensory sensitivity they experience, the more anxious they become – not just at the time, but in between triggering events, because they are afraid something will happen that will trigger the painful build-up to meltdown.

Dr Joliffe (who is on the autistic spectrum) says:

"I live in a state of terror all the time."

Every autistic person is different, and we need to work out which approach will reduce the pressure on their sensory sensitivities.

Speech

Speech is the end product of many processes coming together. It is very complicated to understand and produce. Trying to work out what is being said and then reply increases the stress level.

Almost all autistic people have problems with the two areas in the brain linked to speech: Wernicke's area (understanding written and spoken language) and Broca's area (production of language). These may be damaged or they may not work in sync. What the person may hear is confused. Donna Williams talks about the "blah-blah" of the world.

To answer someone involves many different processes. The nerve cells in Broca's area have to organise the muscles of the tongue and the jaw, shape the mouth and synchronise breathing. Often the person will recognise rhythm and we can float the words on a tune they enjoy.

Overlapping speech and harsh voices are a problem, and people will avoid crowded situations for this reason.

Use a soft, quiet voice. Do not talk to each other over the autistic person.

Bad words and bad feelings

When people on the autistic spectrum do express how they feel, they often say things which upset those who care for them, such as, "I want to hit you" or "I want to kill myself". They may use language that society feels is socially unacceptable, such as "Fuck off!" (meaning "Go away as you are overloading me").

This sort of language expresses how the person really feels, and if we don't align ourselves with this feeling, we are giving them the message that we don't care how they feel.

If someone says, "I want to hit you", answer:

"It really sounds as if you want to hit me."

Their response will be a sigh of relief (like taking the top off a pressure cooker), and they will almost always breathe out:

"Oh, yes, I do."

If you empathise, they will relax: all the anxiety and pain has gone. But you must use the key word to shift their attention away from their inner turmoil and towards the world outside.

With regards to so-called 'bad language', autistic or not, people use swear words to relieve tension. Putting aside what actually constitutes 'bad language' these days and who is using it, the way to help is to respond not by swearing back at them, but by empathising with how they feel. So if they say, "Piss off!" or "Fuck off!", respond:

"*You sound really pissed off / fucked off.*"

They will almost always relax and say:

"*Oh, yes, I am.*"

If we ignore how people feel, we are sending the message that we do not care how they feel. This is particularly important since the autistic person may only be getting their sense of self from how they feel, rather than from mis-wired processing areas. What they need is confirmation that their feelings are real.

(While some care staff may find this approach socially unacceptable, it works. You have to use the key word in order for the person's brain to recognise that there is someone outside themselves who understands how they feel.)

For those who feel doubtful about swearing, an alternative approach (which I have not used personally, but heard about recently) is to have a 'swear list' where you write down the offensive word without having to say it. The care worker was writing each word down using a marker pen, so it was clear that she was paying attention to how the person was feeling. (Success here depends on the autistic person finding written words meaningful.)

Make sure your whole team understands this approach, what you are doing and why. Otherwise, you may get into trouble with people who think you are swearing at the autistic child or adult, or that it will make the habit of 'bad language' worse. Both of these interpretations are wrong.

Trauma

Trauma occurs when we are unable to manage the pain we experience.

By now it should be clear that autism in itself can be traumatic. This is especially true for people who have spent long periods in institutions, where in addition to their sensory issues, physical and sexual abuse have been commonplace.

We have to try to change the brainscript by offering a recognisable alternative for the brain to latch onto when it is upset, so that it can recognise the pattern of our intervention.

Physical feeling of self

Some people say our physical feeling of self is an illusion created by our senses. Whether this is the case or not, it is difficult to know who we are without it.

If we don't have a feeling of embodiment (owning ourselves), it is difficult to define the boundary between 'me' and 'not me' and to know where we are in space. This all contributes to uncertainty and anxiety.

Jim does not stop running around the house, crashing his head against the walls and making noises. When he is confused, it helps him to feel himself. I get his mother to hold him between her knees with a wide belt around his stomach. Every time he makes a sound, she squeezes. This gives him a rhythm that he recognises. He stops trying to pull away and turns to her with a radiant smile. He touches her lips with his finger and looks into her eyes; something he has not done before.

Meg spent much of her childhood in an institution.
She will not come close to anyone. When she is getting
upset, she runs round in a tight circle, muttering:

*"I will be good, I will be good. Don't lock me in the
coal shed."*

As she walks in a tight circle, Meg is banging her
feet. I bang the floor, echoing back to her the rhythm
of her feet. In her sensory confusion, she recognises
the rhythm and it shifts her attention from her inner
turmoil. She comes and sits by me and holds my hand.

WARNING: psychiatric (mis)diagnosis

While addressing sensory issues does not stop the person being autistic, it does improve quality of life and reduce distress behaviour. It is proper to attend to these needs before attempting psychiatric diagnosis.

Psychiatric misdiagnoses can occur when autism and sensory issues are not recognised:

- Mood disorders (e.g., depressive and bipolar-related disorders)

- Anxiety disorders (e.g., Generalised Anxiety Disorder, Social Anxiety Disorder, phobias, Panic Disorder)

- Obsessive-compulsive disorders (e.g., OCD, Hoarding Disorder)

- Disruptive, impulse-control and conduct disorders (e.g., Oppositional Defiant Disorder, Intermittent Explosive Disorder)

- Personality disorders (e.g., Borderline Personality Disorder, Avoidant Personality Disorder)[10]

---

10 See American Psychiatric Association (2013) *Diagnostic and statistical manual of mental disorders: DSM-5*. 5th edn. Washington, D.C.: American Psychiatric Publishing.

Part Two:
Responsive
Communication

A bit of history

In the 1980s, clinical psychologist Geraint Ephraim was feeling frustrated that he could not engage with some people on the autistic spectrum. He was my mentor for four years when I held a Joseph Rowntree Foundation Fellowship. He said:

"Out of sheer desperation one day, I tried copying what an autistic man was doing. To my surprise, he sat up and took notice."

That was the beginning of a practice that Dave Hewett renamed Intensive Interaction: a way of using body language to communicate with people. Intensive Interaction is not 'copying', but tuning in and responding to how the person 'feels' as expressed through their body language.

(Faces and posture give a lot away. There is a difference between an arm waved in greeting and one which expresses defence or aggression. Tune into their mood with empathy.)

However, it's no good trying to interact if you are wearing a brightly-patterned T-shirt which upsets their visual processing. Nowadays, we find it helps to combine Intensive Interaction with addressing sensory issues. This combined style is known as Responsive Communication.

Using body language to communicate

Much of how we communicate with each other is through our body language – one figure puts this at 80% of our personal communication. It tells you how I feel, and me how you feel. Unlike speech, we do this unconsciously.

Speech can tell lies; body language cannot be used to deceive. We feel the disconnection in ourselves and respond to it.

A big man stands over me, bares his teeth in a scary way and almost snarls:

"*I'm mad.*"

But there is something about the way he says it that doesn't quite ring true: his body language is at odds with his words. Without thinking, I hear myself respond to the feeling of mismatch:

"I don't think you are mad, but I think you would like me to think you are mad."

He deflates at once:

"How can you possibly know this since we have only just met?"

First, we must learn to shift our focus from ourselves into the world of our conversation partner. We need to learn to empty our minds of our own concerns.

Mobile phones are a distraction, so, if we are serious, **we put aside our phones while we are working.**

We need to pay our conversation partners 'intimate attention'; not just in terms of what they are doing, but how they are doing it, since this will tell us how they feel. It is one thing to flap your hand gently; another to shake it in an agitated way.

We need to 'listen with all our senses'.

And join in using their body language, since this will have meaning for them.

While we may copy exactly at first, we need to 'learn their language', working out what has meaning for them, so that we can build up a conversation through their hardwired signals that do not need a lot of processing.

('Hardwired' means there is a good connection between the nerve synapses, and the brain does not have to go into overdrive trying to decode the message.)

What has meaning is different for each person, and we need to work out what this is. The clue may be in repetitive behaviour (stimming), which can include particular themes on which the person focuses or subjects in which they are deeply interested. This is what they need to resort to in order to keep confusion at bay, so they have at least one activity that has meaning for them.

I sit next to Sue at a noisy conference. She is doing French knitting to calm herself. I know Sue quite well. She looks at me and laughs, and says:

"*Socially-acceptable stimming?*"

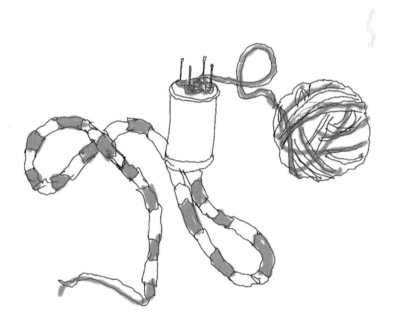

Who says people with autism don't have a sense of humour?

It's not just us reading our conversation partner's body language: because we are using signals they recognise, they will be reading ours.

They will sense fear by smell – and adopt a defensive position.

I tend to sit down (near the door) when I am with someone who is disturbed, since I present as less aggressive than if I am standing and waving my arms around. It is rare to be attacked if you are sitting.

In addition to responding through body language, I use **mime** to support speech and indicate what I am going to do. If I want to go into a room of someone who is in distress, I will stand in the doorway, point to my chest and then into the room and say at the same time:

"May I come in?"

I then wait until they say yes or indicate that it is OK.

I once waited for twenty minutes outside in the rain to enter the room of a very disturbed woman. In the end she let me in and did not attack me. She knew she had control, and I would leave if she needed me to.

If someone hits me, I bang the nearest surface to echo their intent and say I have got their message.

Anticipation

Sometimes when people are getting overloaded – and before they go into meltdown – they will make a recognisable gesture, so their care staff know what is coming.

Before Lizzie pinches staff (hard enough to cause injury and mainly when her neighbour's radio is on too loud and it hurts), she makes a particular facial movement.

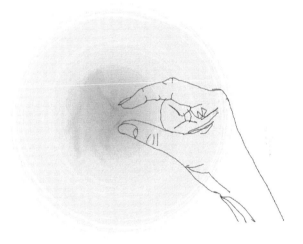

When I spot this, I know she is about to pinch so I give her a firm but gentle squeeze on her arm. This gives her the pressure she needs and indicates to her that I know she is distressed.

She laughs. All her tension has gone.

If we take the lid off our heads and look inside, our brains look like a walnut; the two halves joined by a bridge at the middle, called the corpus callosum.

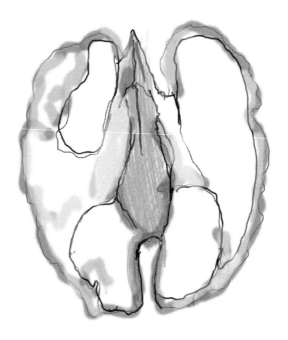

Charlie's brain developed without the band of fibres that join the left and right brains, so there is no contact between them. Thirty per cent of people with corpus callosum damage show autistic features.

Charlie does not understand that what he wants may have consequences; in fact, it is doubtful whether he knows what he wants. (He needs physical objects of reference.)

Charlie loves rhythm and is interested when I use the keyboard to interact with the notes he fingers on the piano. He is interested in the difference between the notes, and also between loud and soft volume, but above all he connects with simple variations of rhythm based on his notes.

I show Charlie's mother how to respond at a lower pitch and softer volume to all his sounds. Once he realises that he will always get a response, communication becomes an open-ended conversation, rather than Charlie just making sounds to talk to himself.

You will know when Charlie is getting upset as he leans on the table. He looks at you, and then beats his head on the hard surface, so you have time to anticipate his self-injury.

When I see him lie his head on the table and know he is about to hurt himself, I pre-empt his self-injury and bang his rhythm before he has time to do it. He stands up immediately, turns his head in my direction, laughs and walks away. He thinks it is funny.

Mike is a big man and easily becomes upset. In particular, he needs confirmation when he comes out of the bathroom after he has cleaned his teeth. He says, "My teeth are white," and if someone does not confirm this he will hit the nearest person.

I suggest to his mother that when the bathroom door starts to open, before he has come out, she says, "Your teeth look nice and white." He thinks this is very funny and his rising anxiety vanishes.

Getting to know you

Finally, we are going to consider a few of the hundreds of interventions that I have carried out with distressed people on the autistic spectrum using body language. If these outcomes seem miraculous, they are not. Rather, they are the careful application of a particular way of working.

Once we get familiar with the actions and words that make up the person's communication style, we can begin to use our shared language more freely (as in conversation) – using their language to divert their attention from their inner distress to a recognisable sound or gesture in the world outside.

We may feel self-conscious when entering the world of our conversation partner, wondering what other people will think of us. If we notice we are doing this, it means we are thinking of ourselves and not our conversation partner, and is a signal that we need to switch our focus.

While the descriptions that follow are helpful, I suggest that readers watch the films of my work with Gabriel and Pranve, both of whom have very severe autism. These are free to view and can be found at www.phoebecaldwell.com/videos

First of all, I look and see what sensory activity has meaning for them: the sensation or activity on which they are focusing.

April

April is about six. She had some speech until she was
three, but has stopped talking since then. I am visiting
April as a result of a letter written by her mother to
the paper asking desperately for help since she fears
April will kill herself. April lives under a blanket.
You can just see her frightened face peeping out.
She makes little sounds. When she is sent to school,
the school send her back, usually within an hour. I
try various ways of attracting her attention without
success, and then notice her fingers are scratching
the edge of the blanket. When she is scratching, she
knows what she is doing.

Every time April scratches, therefore, I scratch back, using the same rhythm. She notices almost at once and becomes more alert. After about five minutes, she pushes her blanket tent back, and starts to smile. I start to gently scratch her fingers directly. She comes out. At this stage I decide to use vibration to give a bigger boost to her self-stimulation. We make a game of 'swapping' two electric toothbrushes; the only vibrating items I have with me. By now, she is right out of her tent, laughing and playing with me on the sofa. Her mother is open-mouthed with astonishment.

April's grandmother phones while my colleague and I have gone out for lunch. April grabs the phone and tells her she wants cottage cheese for lunch. That night when she is being put to bed, there is a noise in the street. April says,

"*What a noise!*"

Her mother continues to use this approach. April is able to return to school, and when I last heard she was coping well.

Josh

When Josh is upset, he beats his head on the wall. I respond with the rhythm of his bangs, and he stops and looks at me. (*That's a rhythm I recognise but it is coming from outside.*) Although he does not speak, he is a very able young man and uses his computer to communicate. A friend asks him if he doesn't find it patronising to have someone imitate him. He replies (via his computer) that on the contrary, it is like having a "delicious conversation" when he is upset.[11]

---

11 Caldwell, P. (2012) *Delicious Conversations: Reflections on autism, intimacy and communication.* Pavilion Publishing and Media Ltd.

Gabriel

Gabriel[12] is autistic. He lives in a large residential home. He has epilepsy and struggles to make sense of the world. He crashes into the kitchen and wanders around banging his head.

Care staff give him biscuits to calm him. He wanders around picking up objects, feeling things and dropping them. When I am in his way, he pushes me aside – not aggressively, but as if I were a piece of furniture. People mean nothing to him.

12 www.phoebecaldwell.com/videos

I try a number of ways of getting Gabriel's attention without success.

Eventually he sits on the floor with a pair of rubber gloves and flicks them onto his left wrist.

I sit with him and do the same, and he begins to look at what I am doing. He picks up some string and gradually realises that if he makes a movement, I will respond.

Gabriel starts to smile and make a deliberate movement, and then look at me and wait for my response. Now we are engaged in a shared conversation.

We progress through a number of activities until eventually he does something completely new: banging the sink and looking to see if I will respond. He is radiant when I do, and looks around the room at the other people to share his pleasure with them.

Pranve

Pranve[13] lives beside Heathrow airport.

13   www.phoebecaldwell.com/videos

Pranve is afraid of the sound of passing planes and attacks his mother frequently. I have been warned he will attack me or run away, so when his mother opens the door, I stand outside, listen, and hear a repeated sound from upstairs:

"*Er-Er-Er.*"

So I answer in the same vein, but using the rhythm of words I might have used ("Hello. Here I am."): "Er-er, er-er-er?", lifting my voice on the third syllable so that it sounds as though I am asking a question.

To my surprise, Pranve appears, takes my hand and leads me into the sitting room. He sits down and plays with his fingers. I ask Pranve if I may sit down, accompanying my request with a gesture pointing to the sofa beside his armchair. He points to the chair, so I know he has understood. I sit down.

Sitting half-turned away and glancing up at the planes, Pranve's body language still indicates anxiety. He continues to make "Er-er-er" sounds, which I answer empathetically. (These derive from the rhythm of syllables in the only thing he has ever been known to say: "Where's Charlene?" Charlene is Pranve's sister, who has moved to live with her aunt as he was attacking her.)

Next, Pranve produces a ball of string. He gives it to me momentarily, and then takes it back and tucks it away. At this point, he decides that I no longer represent a threat and turns towards me, smiling and engaging with eye contact.

I begin to tap the rhythms of Pranve's sounds onto his chair, and next onto his arm. This is so successful that I become overconfident and place my hand on his when he is not looking, so he is unaware of what I am going to do. He draws back immediately and thumps my arm; not badly, but enough to show me that he cannot cope with unexpected events.

Pranve then goes into an anxiety routine that I do not read correctly at the time. He touches the fringe on a standard lamp between his chair and my sofa and then runs his hand down the upright stand. He then takes my hand and tries to get me to do the same. I flick the fringe but miss out the stand. I just do not see the significance of this until looking at the film afterwards. My failure to pick up on this leads to our first session being cut short.

After lunch, our next session starts with Pranve kneeling in the hall and banging the door. His father says he does this when he is angry, and they try to stop him. I suggest that rather than stopping him we need to answer, so every time he bangs, I respond by stamping. He is now getting a response that is contingent but slightly different, although similar enough to recognise. He starts to laugh, throwing his ball of string into the room as a strategy to get himself back from the hall into the sitting room to reclaim it. He comes in, picks up the string and stamps as I had. I stamp again. He looks up, spots his mother and goes over and kisses her for the first time ever.

Pravne's father observes that they had been trying to control him, whereas I was always with him.

In the last session, Pranve starts to hum. It is clear that he knows what he wants to do. First of all he gets the rhythms, then the pitch and finally the words. We can see his head moving round, literally 'getting his head around it', as he tries to show us. His jaw wobbles with the effort. To the amazement of his family and the speech therapist, he comes out with 'Baa, Baa, Black Sheep': something they have never heard before. Some might see this as inappropriate for Pranve's age, but we could see how delighted he was that he had managed it – and we were delighted for him.

When it is time to leave, Pranve has gone to sit in his room in a bay window. Since his body language is conveying that he needs space, I go round to the outside of the house and splay my hand on the window close to him to say 'goodbye'. He looks at his right hand which was resting on his knee, carefully unrolls it, splays his fingers out and brings it up to cover mine on the other side of the glass.

A month later his mother phones:

"He is much better. While he still has his off days, we know how to engage with him now and he is able to go back to his day centre."

Sadly, Pranve died six months later, when he had a severe seizure and the ambulance was sent to the wrong address. His ashes were taken back to India and scattered in the river Ganges.

Respecting difference

April, Josh, Gabriel and Pranve are people who became friends. But long-term change in the quality of an individual's life is dependent on our continuing to use body language with them – not just occasionally, but as the first way of communicating. This will change as the autistic person gains in confidence. We have to be a ladder, offering them a way out of their locked-in world. **We must not miss it if they introduce something new, as this will mean we are not attending to them and we will lose their confidence.**

We talk about respect for the individual, but much of what is on offer is tuned to how we think they ought to be, rather than how they truly are in themselves.

Over the last fifty years I have been privileged to meet and engage with (and show others how to engage with) all these people and many more.

First and foremost, we need to see if we can help with any sensory difficulties that are making information processing difficult.

Distress behaviour fades as we enter the colourful new dimension of communicating through feeling. Emotional engagement changes our partners' lives and our own. It is a big step: try it and see.

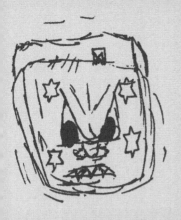

The ANGeR Box

Sensory turmoil and pain in autism

By Phoebe Caldwell

In her best-selling book, Phoebe Caldwell, an expert practitioner with over 30 years' experience working with people with learning disabilities, offers us a fresh insight into autism spectrum disorders (ASD).

Shifting the attention away from presentation and symptoms alone, Phoebe explores and attempts to understand the sensory issues experienced by those on the spectrum and their neurobiological roots in an effort to find new ways of alleviating the distress that can characterise this condition.

The Anger Box explores the relationship between pain and external stimuli, trigeminal neuralgia, visual distortions, sensory overload, environmental and neurological factors implicated in the development of ASD, and a wide range of other areas.

Drawing upon her own wealth of experience, the experiences of people on the spectrum and new scientific research, Phoebe presents a fascinating and engaging exploration of life on the spectrum, richly textured, vibrant and above all informative.

Who will this book benefit?

The Anger Box will be of interest to professionals, parents with autistic children, those with a general interest in the subject and many individuals on the autism spectrum themselves.

Find out more and buy online:
www.pavpub.com/the-anger-box

£12.95 | Handbook | 978-1-909810-44-0

Responsive
Communication

Combining attention to sensory issues with
using body language (Intensive Interaction)
to interact with autistic adults and children

Digital version now available

Responsive Communication is an approach that combines
using body language (Intensive Interaction) with attention
to sensory issues to help achieve meaningful interaction with
autistic people and people with profound and multiple learning
disabilities. Responsive Communication is an effective means of
emotionally engaging with and reducing behavioural distress of
these individuals.

The authors offer a range of informative perspectives on the
approach and application of Responsive Communication,
from backgrounds including expert by experience, speech and
language therapy, service management, occupational therapy,
autism practitioner, neuroscience and psychiatry.

Find out more and buy online:
www.pavpub.com/learning-disability/autism/
responsive-communication

£24.95 | 204pp | Paperback | 978-1-912755-36-3

Maybugs
and
Mortality

A different perspective on living and ageing

Maybugs and Mortality is a unique 'monograph for two' about key aspects of the shared latter lifecycles of a maybug and us humans, and the physical and psychological differences between having an internal or an external skeleton. In this semi-autobiographical account, the author rides in tandem with her companion, 'Maybugs'. From this unusual parallel, themes such as consciousness, self-awareness and the need to reach out beyond ourselves to find confirmation and understanding are explored.

'While I do not think I actually like insects, Maybugs comes with a wealth of stories – if the flight path is erratic, the destination is fascinating. I have learned respect and at times, felt an odd affection for my fellow traveller.' (Phoebe Caldwell)

In this light-hearted book, Phoebe draws upon her work and experience of autism to examine what we mean when we talk about boundaries and the difference between 'me' and 'not me'.

Maybugs and Mortality is an intriguing and informative read for anyone who is interested in human behaviour, psychology and autism.

Find out more and buy online:
www.pavpub.com/health-and-social-care/ health-autism/maybugs-mortality

£15.95 | 104pp | Paperback | 978-1-912755-21-9